The Loneliness of the Dying

Norbert Elias

THE LONELINESS
OF THE DYING

Translated by Edmund Jephcott

Basil Blackwell

English edition first published 1985
First published in paperback 1986
Reprinted 1987

Basil Blackwell Ltd
108 Cowley Road, Oxford OX4 1JF, UK

Basil Blackwell Inc.
432 Park Avenue South, Suite 1503,
New York, NY 10016, USA

British Library Cataloguing in Publication Data

Elias, Norbert
   The loneliness of the dying.
   1. Death — Social aspects
   I. Title   II. Uber die Einsamkeit der
   Sterbenden. *English*
   306.9'09   HQ1073
   ISBN 0-631-13902-8
   ISBN 0-631-15058-7 Pbk

Library of Congress Cataloging in Publication Data

Elias, Norbert.
   The loneliness of the dying.
   Includes index.
   1. Death.   I. Title.
   BD444.E4413 1985   128'.5   84-24586
   ISBN 0-631-13902-8
   ISBN 0-631-15058-7 (pbk.)

Typeset by Getset (BTS) Ltd, Eynsham, Oxford
Printed in the USA

Contents

The main text was first published in German in 1982. The postscript is a revised version of a lecture delivered at a medical congress at Bad Salzuflen in October 1983.

1

THERE are various ways of dealing with the fact that all lives, including those of the people we love, have an end. The end of human life, which we call death, can be mythologized through the idea of an afterlife in Hades or Valhalla, in Hell or Paradise. This is the oldest and commonest form of the human endeavour to come to terms with the finiteness of life. We can attempt to avoid the thought of death by pushing it as far from ourselves as possible – by hiding and repressing the unwelcome idea – or by holding an unshakable belief in our own personal immortality – 'others die, I do not'. There is a strong tendency towards this in the advanced societies of our day. Finally, we can look death in the face as a fact of our own existence; we can adjust our lives, and particularly our behaviour towards other people, to the limited span of every life. We might see it as our task to make the end, the parting from human beings, when it comes, as easy and as pleasant as possible, for others as for ourselves; and we might pose the question of how this task is to be performed. At present this is a question that is being asked in a clear, unclouded way only by a number of doctors – in the broader debate of society the question is hardly raised.

And this is not merely a question of the actual

termination of life, the death certificate and the urn. Many people die gradually; they grow infirm, they age. The last hours are important, of course. But often the parting begins much earlier. Their frailty is often enough to sever the ageing from the living. Their decline isolates them. They may grow less sociable, their feelings less warm, without their need for people being extinguished. That is the hardest thing — the tacit isolation of the ageing and dying from the community of the living, the gradual cooling of their relationships to people to whom they were attached, the separation from human beings in general, who gave them meaning and security. The declining years are hard not only for those in pain, but for those who are left alone. The fact that, without being specifically intended, the early isolation of the dying occurs with particular frequency in the more advanced societies is one of the weaknesses of these societies. It bears witness to the difficulties that many people have of identifying with the ageing and dying.

No doubt the scope of identification is wider than in earlier times. We no longer regard it as a Sunday entertainment to see people hanged, quartered, broken on the wheel. We watch football, not gladiatorial contests. As compared with antiquity, our identification with other people, our sharing in their suffering and death, has increased. To watch hungry lions and tigers devouring living people piece by piece, or gladiators trying by ruse and deceit to wound and murder each other, is scarcely a diversion that we would anticipate with the same relish as the Roman senators decked in purple, or the Roman people. No feeling of identity, it seems, united those spectators with these other people who, below in the bloody arena, were fighting for their lives. As we know, the gladiators greeted the caesar as they marched in with the words, 'Morituri te salutant.'[1] Some of the caesars doubtless believed themselves actually immortal, like the gods. At all events, it would have been more appropriate had the gladiators shouted: 'Morituri moriturum salutant.'[2] But in a society where it would have been possible to say that, there probably would have been no gladiators or caesars. To be able to say that to the rulers — some of whom even today have power of life and death over countless of their fellows — requires a more extensive de-mythologization of death than has been achieved so far, and a much clearer awareness that humankind is a community of mortals, and that people in their need can expect help only from people. The social problem of death is especially difficult to solve because the living find it hard to identify with the dying.

Death is a problem of the living. Dead people have no problems. Of the many creatures on this earth that die, it is human beings alone for whom dying is a problem. They share birth, illness, youth, maturity, age and death with the animals. But they alone of all living beings *know* that they shall die; they alone can anticipate their own end, are aware that it can come at any time, and take special precautions — as individuals and as groups — to protect themselves against

[1] 'Those about to die salute you.'
[2] 'Those who are going to die salute him who is going to die.'

3

the danger of annihilation.

Through the millenia this was a central function of human groupings such as tribes or states, and it has remained a main function to this day. However, among the greatest dangers to humans are humans. In the name of their aim of protecting themselves from destruction, groups of people again and again threaten other groups with destruction. From the earliest days, societies formed by human beings have been Janus-faced: inward pacification, outward threat. In other species, too, the survival value of societies has found expression in the formation of groups and in the adjustment of individuals to group-life as a permanent feature of their existence. But in their case, the adjustment to group-life is based largely on genetically predetermined forms of conduct or, at the most, on small learned variations of innate behaviour. In the case of human beings the balance between unlearned and learned adjustment to group-life has been reversed. Innate dispositions to a life with others require activation through learning – the disposition to speak, for instance, through learning a language. Human beings not only can, but must, learn to regulate conduct with each other in terms of group-specific constraints or rules. Without learning they are not able to function as individuals and group-members. Nowhere has this attunement to life in groups had such a profound influence on the form and development of the individual as in the human species. Not only means of communication or patterns of constraint, but the experience of death, too, can differ from society to society. It is variable

4

and group-specific; no matter how natural and immutable it seems to the members of each particular society, it has been learned.

It is not actually death, but the knowledge of death, that creates problems for human beings. We should not be deceived: the fly caught between a person's fingers struggles as convulsively as a human being in the clutches of a murderer, as if it knows the peril it is in. But the fly's defensive movements when in mortal danger are an unlearned gift of its species. A mother monkey may carry her dead offspring for a while before dropping it somewhere and losing it. She knows nothing of death, either her child's or her own. Human beings know, and so for them death becomes a problem.

2

THE answer to the question as to the nature of death changes in the course of social development. It is stage-specific. Within each stage it is also group-specific. Ideas of death and the attendant rituals themselves become an aspect of socialization. Common ideas and rites unite people; divergent ones separate groups. It would be worthwhile to present a survey of all the beliefs that people have held in the course of centuries in order to come to terms with the problem of death and its incessant threat to their lives; and at the same time to give an account of all they have done to each other in the name of a belief that promised that death was not an end, that the

5

rituals attending it could secure them eternal life. Clearly there is no notion, however bizarre, in which people are not prepared to believe with profound devotion, provided it gives them relief from the knowledge that one day they will not exist, provided it gives them hope in a form of eternal existence.

Undoubtedly, in advanced societies groups of people no longer insist so passionately that only their own supernatural belief and its rites can secure for their members an eternal life after the earthly one. In the Middle Ages people with minority beliefs were frequently pursued with fire and sword. On a crusade against the Albigenses in southern France in the thirteenth century, a stronger community of believers wiped out a weaker one. Its members were stigmatized, driven from their homes and burned at the stake in hundreds. 'With joy in our hearts we watched them burn,' said one of the victors. No feeling of identity between humans and humans here; belief and ritual divided them. With expulsion, prison, torture and burnings, the Inquisition carried on the campaign of the Crusaders against people of different beliefs. The religious wars of the early modern period are well enough known. Their aftermath is still felt today, for example in Ireland. The recent struggle between priests and secular rulers in Persia also reminds us of the passionate ferocity of communal feeling and the enmity that supernatural systems of belief were able to unleash in medieval societies, because they promised redemption from death, and eternal life.

In the more developed societies, as I have said, the

search for help against danger and death in systems of supernatural belief has become somewhat less passionate; it has to an extent shifted its base to secular systems of belief. The need for guarantees against one's own transience has abated perceptibly in recent centuries as compared with the Middle Ages, reflecting a different stage of civilization. In the more developed nation-states people's security, their protection against the more brutal strokes of fate such as illness and sudden death, is much greater than in earlier periods, and perhaps greater than at any time in the development of humanity. As compared with earlier stages, life in these societies has become more predictable, while demanding from each individual a higher degree of foresight and control of the passions. The relatively high life expectancy of individuals in these societies is a reflection of the increased security. Among the knights of the thirteenth century a man of forty was counted almost an old man; in the industrial societies of the twentieth century he is considered almost young — with class-specific differences. The prevention and treatment of illness in the present century are better organized than ever before, inadequate as they may still be. The internal pacification of society, the individual's protection against violence not sanctioned by the state, as against starvation, has reached a pitch unimaginable to people of earlier times.

Of course, on closer inspection we see by way of correction how great the individual's insecurity in this world still is. And the drift towards war brings a constant threat into the lives of individuals. Only

7

from a somewhat long-range perspective, by comparison with earlier times, do we realize how much our security against unforeseeable physical dangers and incalculable threats to our existence has increased. It appears that the attachment to otherworldly beliefs that promise metaphysical protection from the blows of fate, and above all from personal transience, is most passionate in those classes and groups whose lives are most uncertain and least under their own control. But, by and large, in developed societies the dangers threatening people, particularly that of death, are more predictable, while the need for protective superhuman powers has grown more temperate. One cannot doubt that, with increasing social uncertainty, and with the decreasing ability of people to foresee and – to an extent – control their own fate over long periods, these needs would grow stronger again.

The attitude to dying and the image of death in our societies cannot be completely understood without reference to this relative security and predictability of individual life and the correspondingly increased life expectancy. Life grows longer, death is further postponed. The sight of dying and dead people is no longer commonplace. It is easier in the normal course of life to forget death. Death is sometimes said to be 'repressed'. An American coffin-manufacturer observed recently: 'The present-day attitude to death leaves planning for a funeral, if it happens at all, to late in life.'[3]

[3] B. Deborah Frazier, 'Your Coffin as Furniture – For Now', *International Herald Tribune*, 2 October 1979.

3

IF death is nowadays said to be 'repressed', it seems to me that the term is used in a double sense. A 'repression' on both the individual and social planes can be meant. In the first case, the term is used in much the same way as by Freud. It refers to a whole group of socially instilled psychological defence mechanisms by which excessively painful childhood experiences, particularly conflicts in early childhood and the associated guilt and anxiety, are denied access to memory. In indirect and disguised ways they influence a person's feelings and behaviour; but they have vanished from memory.

Early childhood experiences and fantasies also play a considerable part in the way a person comes to terms with the knowledge of his or her approaching death. Some people can look towards their death with serenity, others have a powerful, constant fear of death, often without expressing it or being able to do so. They are perhaps aware of it only as of a fear of flying or of open spaces. A familiar way of making strong childhood anxieties relating to death bearable without having come to terms with them is to imagine oneself immortal. This takes many forms. I know people who are not able to have anything to do with dying people because their compensatory fantasy of immortality, which holds their overwhelming infantile fears in check, is weakened alarmingly by the proximity of the dying. This weakening could allow their powerful fear of death — of punishment — to enter consciousness more nakedly, which would be unbearable.

We find here, in an extreme form, one of the more general problems of our day — our inability to give dying people the help and affection they are most in need of when parting from other human beings, just because another's death is a reminder of our own. The sight of a dying person shakes the defensive fantasies that people are apt to build like a wall against the idea of their own death. Self-love whispers that they are immortal: too-close contact with the dying threatens the wish-dream. Behind an overwhelming need to believe in one's own immortality, and so deny the foreknowledge of one's own death, there usually lie strong repressed guilt feelings, perhaps connected to death-wishes directed at father, mother or siblings, with the concomitant fear of being wished dead by them. In this case the only escape from the guilt-anxiety surrounding the death-wish, particularly when directed at family members, and from the idea of their revenge, the fear of punishment for one's guilt, is a particularly strong belief in one's own immortality, even though one may be partly aware of the fragility of this belief.

The association of the fear of death with guilt-feelings is already to be found in ancient myths. In paradise Adam and Eve were immortal. God condemned them to die because Adam, the man, had violated the commandment of the divine father. The feeling, too, that death is a punishment imposed on women and men by a father or mother figure, or that after death they will be punished by the great father

10

for their sins, has played a not inconsiderable part in the human fear of death over a long period. It would certainly be possible to make dying easier for some people if repressed guilt-fantasies of this kind could be alleviated or dispelled.

But hand in hand with these individual problems of the repression of the idea of death go specific social problems. On this plane the concept of repression has a different meaning. However, the peculiarity of the behaviour towards death prevalent in society today is perceived only when this behaviour is compared with that of earlier times or of other societies. Only then can one place the change of behaviour to be observed here in a wider theoretical framework, and so make it more accessible to explanation. To state the matter straight away, the change in social behaviour referred to by speaking of the 'repression' of death in this sense is an aspect of the more comprehensive civilizing spurt that I have examined in more detail elsewhere.[4] In its course all elementary, animal aspects of human life, which almost without exception spell danger for the communal life of people as for the individual himself, are regulated more evenly, more inescapably and in a more differentiated way than before by social rules and by conscience as well. In accordance with changing power relationships, they become associated with feelings of shame, repugnance or embarrassment, and in certain cases, especially in the great European spurt of civilization, they are banished behind the scenes or at any rate

[4] Cf. Norbert Elias, *The Civilizing Process*, vol. 1, New York, 1978, vol. 2, Oxford, 1982; particularly vol. 2, pp. 229ff.

11

removed from public social life. The long-term change in the behaviour of people towards the dying follows the same direction. Death is one of the great bio-social dangers in human life. Like other animal aspects, death, both as a process and as memory-image, is pushed more and more behind the scenes of social life during this civilizing spurt. For the dying themselves this means that they too are pushed further behind the scenes, are isolated.

4

PHILIPPE Ariès, in his very stimulating and well-documented book *Studien zur Geschichte des Todes im Abendland* ('A History of Death in the West'), has attempted to give his readers a vivid picture of the changes undergone in the behaviour and attitudes of Western people towards death. But Ariès understands history purely as description. He accumulates image after image and so in broad strokes shows the total change. This is fine and stimulating, but it explains nothing. Ariès's selection of facts is based on a preconceived opinion. He tries to convey his assumption that in earlier times people died serenely and calmly. It is only in the present, he postulates, that things are different. In a Romantic spirit Ariès looks mistrustfully on the bad present in the name of a better past. Rich as his book is in historical evidence, his selection and interpretation of the evidence has to be approached with great caution. It is difficult to follow him when he adduces the

Romans de la Table Ronde, the conduct of Isolde and Archbishop Turpin, as evidence of how calmly medieval people awaited death. He does not point out that these medieval epics are idealizations of knightly life, selective wishful images that often throw more light on what the poet and his audience thought it ought to be than on what it was. The same applies to other literary sources used by Ariès. His conclusion is characteristic and shows his partiality:

> Thus [that is, calmly] did people die in the course of centuries or millennia. . . . This ancient attitude, for which death was familiar, close and softened, indifferent in one, contrasts abruptly to our own, in which death arouses fear in us to the point that we no longer dare to call it by its name. This is why I call that familiar death *tamed death*. I do not mean by that that it had *earlier* been wild. . . . I mean, on the contrary, that it has become wild *today*.[5]

As compared with life in highly industrialized nation-states, life in medieval feudal states was — and is, wherever such states still exist in the present — passionate, violent, and therefore uncertain, brief and wild. Dying can be full of torment and pain. In earlier times people had fewer possibilities of alleviating the torment. Not even today has the art of medicine advanced sufficiently to ensure a painless death for everyone. But it is great enough to allow a more peaceful death for many people who would earlier have died in dreadful agony.

[5] Philippe Ariès, *Studien zur Geschichte des Todes im Abendland*, Munich/Vienna, 1976, p. 25.

13

What is certain is that death and dying were spoken of more openly and frequently in the Middle Ages than is the case today. The popular literature of the time bears witness to this. Dead people, or Death in person, appear in many poems. In one, three living people pass an open grave and the dead tell them: 'What you are, we have been. What we are, you will be.' In another, Life and Death are having a dispute. Life complains that Death is trampling on her children; Death boasts of his successes. In comparison with the present, death at that time was, for young and old, less concealed, more pervasive, more familiar. This does not mean that it was more peaceful. And the social level of the fear of death was not constant throughout the many centuries of the Middle Ages. It rose noticeably in the course of the fourteenth century. The towns grew. The plague became more stubborn and swept in great waves across Europe. People were afraid of the death all around them. Preachers and mendicant friars intensified the fear. In pictures and writings emerged the motif of the dances of death, the *danses macabres*. Peaceful death in the past? What a one-sided historical perspective! It would not be without interest to compare the social level of the fear of death in our days, in the context of environmental pollution and atomic weapons, to the social level of fear at earlier stages of civilization, with less internal pacification within states and less control of epidemics and other diseases.

What was sometimes comforting and helpful for the dying in the past was the presence of other people.

14

But this depended on their attitude. We are told[6] that Thomas More, Chancellor to Henry VIII, embraced his dying father on his deathbed and kissed him on the mouth — a father whom he had revered and respected throughout his life. There were other cases when the heirs standing around the bed mocked and taunted the dying old man. It all depended on the people concerned. Considered as a stage of social development, the Middle Ages were an exceedingly restless period. Violence was more commonplace, conflict more impassioned, war was often the rule and peace the exception. Epidemics swept across the Eurasian landmass, thousands died in torment and squalor without help or comfort. Bad harvests made bread scarce for the poor every few years. Crowds of beggars and cripples were a normal feature of the medieval landscape. People were capable of great kindness as they were of naked cruelty, unconcealed joy in the torment of others and total indifference to their distress. The contrasts were sharper than today — both between an unbridled sating of the appetites and unbridled self-abasement, asceticism and penance under the weight of a terryifying sense of sin, and between the splendour of the lords and the wretchedness of the poor. Fear of punishment after death, anxiety about the salvation of the soul, often seized rich and poor alike without warning. Princes, to be on the safe side, founded churches, and

[6] William Roper, *The Life of Sir Thomas More*, London, 1969. But see also my critical observations on Roper's reliability: 'Thomas Morus' Staatskritik', in *Utopieforschung*, vol. 2, ed. Wilhelm Voßkamp, Stuttgart, 1982, pp. 101–50, especially pp. 137–44.

monasteries; the poor prayed and repented.

Ariès, as far as I can see, says little about the fear of hell fostered by the Church. But there are medieval pictures that show what, according to the ideas of the time, awaited people after death. An example can still be found in a famous cemetery from the late Middle Ages at Pisa. There a picture vividly depicts the terrors awaiting people after death. It shows the angels leading the saved souls to endless life in paradise, and the horrible demons tormenting the damned in hell. With such terrifying images before the eyes a peaceful death cannot have been easy.

All in all, life in this medieval society was shorter, the dangers less controllable, dying often more painful, the sense of guilt and the fear of punishment after death an official doctrine; but, for better or for worse, the participation of others in an individual's death was far more normal. Today we know how to alleviate the pains of death in some cases; guilt-anxieties are more fully repressed, perhaps even mastered. Religious bodies are less able to buttress their rule by the fear of hell. But the involvement of others in an individual's death has diminished. As with other aspects of a civilizing process, it is not quite easy to balance gains against costs. But the black-and-white picture painted by the feeling, 'good past, bad present', serves little purpose. The primary question is how it was and why it was so and why it has become different. Once we are sure of the answers to these questions, we may be in a position to form a value-judgement.

5

IN the course of a civilizing process the problems faced by people change. But they do not change in a structureless, chaotic way. On close inspection we detect a specific order even in the succession of human–social problems accompanying such a process. These problems too have forms specific to their particular stage.

So, for example, people became aware of virus diseases as a separate problem only after they had succeeded in explaining, and to some extent controlling, the great bacterial infections. The gain was not in vain, as it represented progress, but it was not absolute, as it did not end the struggle with pathogenic agents. The same is true of population growth. Progress in the fight against disease, particularly the curbing of the great epidemics, is partly responsible for this blind, unplanned and dangerous process. What should we think of someone who, faced by this danger of a population explosion, longed for a return to the 'better past' with its Malthusian restraints on population growth – plague, war, abstinence, hunger and early death?

In the course of the marked civilization spurt that set in four or five hundred years ago, people's attitudes to death, and the manner of dying itself, underwent a change, along with many other things. The main outline and direction of this change is quite unambiguous. It can be demonstrated through a few examples, even in a context where it is not possible to do justice to the complex structure of this change.

In earlier times dying was a far more public matter than it is today. This could not be otherwise, first of all because it was far less usual for people to be alone. Nuns and monks may have been alone in their cells, but ordinary people lived constantly together. The dwellings left them little choice. Birth and death – like other animal aspects of human life – were more public, and thus also more sociable, events than today; they were less privatized. Nothing is more characteristic of the present-day attitude to death than the reluctance of adults to make children acquainted with the facts of death. This is particularly note-worthy as a symptom of the repression of death on the individual and the social planes. A vague feeling that children might be harmed causes people to hide from them the simple facts of life that they must inevitably come to know and understand. But the danger for children does not lie in their knowing of the finiteness of every human life, including their father's and mother's and their own; children's fantasies in any case revolve around this problem, and the fear and anxiety surrounding it are frequently intensified by the passionate power of their imaginations. The awareness that they normally have a long life before them can, in contrast to their disturbing fantasies, be actually beneficial. The difficulty lies in how children are told about death, rather than in what they are told. Adults who shy away from talking to their children about death feel, perhaps not without reason, that they might communicate their own anxieties to the children. I know of cases where one parent has been killed in a car accident. The children's reactions depend on their age and their personality structure, but the deeply traumatic effect that such an experience can have on them makes me believe that it would be salutory for children to become acquainted as a matter of course with the simple fact of death, the finitness of their own lives as of all others. Undoubtedly, the aversion of adults today to teaching children the biological facts of death is a peculiarity of the dominant pattern of civilization at this stage. In former days, children too were present when people died. Where everything happens in large measure before the eyes of others, dying also takes place in front of children.

6

AT the preceding stages of social development, people were less evenly restrained all round in the sphere of social life, including speech, thought and writings. The personal censor, and that of one's fellows, took a different form. A poem from a relatively late period – the seventeenth century – may help to illustrate the difference. It is by the Silesian poet Christian Hofmann von Hofmannswaldau, and bears the title, 'Transience of Beauty'.

> Pallid death shall with his chilly hand
> At last, with time, your breasts caress;

The lovely coral of your lips shall pale
The snow of your warm shoulders turn cold sand
Your eyes' sweet flash / the vigour of your hand
For whom they fall / they early shall give way
Your hair / that now attains the sheen of gold
The years at last uproot, a common skein
Your well-shaped foot / your movements' grace
Shall be part dust / part nothingness and void
Then none shall worship more your splendour now
   divine,
This and still more than this at last shall pass away
Your heart alone for all time can endure
Because of diamond Nature it has made.

Readers of our day may find the metaphor of pallid death caressing the breasts of the beloved with his cold hand somewhat crass, perhaps in bad taste. They may, on the contrary, see in the poem a deep concern with the problem of death. But perhaps it is only on account of a singular spurt of informalization, which started after 1918, was sharply reversed in 1933 and then again gathered momentum from 1945 on, that it is possible to concern ourselves with this poem. Like many Baroque poems, it offends against a large number of Victorian and Wilhelmine taboos. To refer in such detail, so unromantically and even somewhat jocularly, to the beloved's death may even today, in the prevailing mild thaw of Victorian taboos, seem somewhat unusual. Until one takes account of the civilizatory changes that find expression in the present day, and thus in one's own personality structure, one shall remain in the dark as interpreter, as hermeneutic historian of the past. Arbitrary interpretations will be the norm, wrong conclusions the rule. The fact that earlier generations spoke more openly of death, the grave and worms is likely to be taken as an indication of their morbid interest in death, their frank references to the physical relations between men and women as signs of prurience or loose morals. Only when we become capable of greater detachment from ourselves, from our own stage of civilization, and aware of the stage-specific character of our own threshold of shame and repugnance, can we do justice to the actions and works of people of other stages.

A poem like this one probably arose far more directly from the social intercourse of men and women than do the more private and individualized poems of our time. In it seriousness and wit are combined in a way that is scarcely paralleled today. Perhaps it was a poem written for a particular occasion; it may have circulated in Hofmannswaldau's circles and caused much amusement to his friends of both sexes. The solemn or sentimental tone that was later often linked with reminders of death and the grave is lacking here. That such an admonition is actually combined with a joke shows the difference of attitude especially clearly. People in the poet's circle will have enjoyed a joke that easily eludes a modern reader. Hofmannswaldau tells his reluctant beloved that all her beauty will vanish in the grave, her coral lips, her snow-white shoulders, her flashing eyes, her whole body will decay — except her heart: that is hard as a diamond, since she will not listen to his pleas. In the register of contemporary feelings there is scarcely anything corresponding to this mixture of

21

the funereal and the flippant, this detailed description of human decomposition as a manoeuvre of flirtation.

One might perhaps take this poem to be the individual invention of its writer. From a literary–historical viewpoint it can be too easily interpreted in this way. But in the present context, as evidence of the attitude to death existing at a different stage of civilization, the poem takes its significance precisely from the fact that its theme is anything but an individual invention. It is a common theme of European Baroque poetry in the widest sense, which conveys to us something of the manner of the love games in the courtly–patrician societies of the seventeenth century. In these societies there were numerous poems on the same theme. Only its poetic treatment was individual and variable. The most beautiful and most famous poem on this theme is Marvell's 'To his Coy Mistress'. It contains the same blunt reminder of what awaits the lovely body in the grave, admonishing the hard-hearted woman not to make him wait so long. This poem, too, was unregarded for centuries. Today, lines from it are favourite anthology quotations:

> The grave's a fine and private place,
> But none, I think, do there embrace.

Variations on the same theme are found in Ronsard, Opitz and other poets of the period. It represents a different threshold of shame and embarrassment from our own, and so a different, social personality structure, not an isolated individual. Reference to death, the grave and all the detailed things that hap-

22

pen to dead human beings there was not subjected to such strict social censorship. The sight of decaying human bodies was more commonplace. Everyone, including children, knew what they looked like; and because everybody knew, they could be spoken of relatively freely, in society and in poetry.

Today things are different. Never before in the history of humanity have the dying been removed so hygienically behind the scenes of social life; never before have human corpses been expedited so odourlessly and with such technical perfection from the deathbed to the grave.

7

C LOSELY bound up, in our day, with the greatest possible exclusion of death and dying from social life, and with the screening-off of dying people from others, from children in particular, is a peculiar embarrassment felt by the living in the presence of dying people. They often do not know what to say. The range of words available for use in this situation is relatively narrow. Feelings of embarrassment hold words back. For the dying this can be a bitter experience. While still alive, they are already deserted. But even here, the problem that dying and death poses for those left behind does not exist in isolation. The reticence and lack of spontaneity in expressing feelings of sympathy in the critical situations of other people is not limited to the presence of someone who is dying or in mourning. At our stage of civilization it manifests itself on many occasions that demand the expression of strong emotional participation without loss of self-control. It is similar with situations of love and tenderness.

In all such cases it is especially the younger generations that, more than in earlier centuries, are forced back on their own resources, their own individual powers of invention, in seeking the right words for their feelings. Social tradition provides individual people with fewer stereotyped expressions or standardized forms of behaviour that might make it easier to meet the emotional demands of such situations. Conventional phrases and rituals are, of course, still in use, but more people than earlier feel uneasy using them, because they seem shallow and worn-out. The ritual formulae of the old society, which made it easier to cope with critical life-situations such as this, sound stale and insincere to many young people; new rituals reflecting the current standard of feeling and behaviour, which might make it easier to cope with the recurrent crises in life, do not yet exist.

It would give a false picture to suggest that the stage-specific problems in the relation of the healthy to the dying, the living to the dead, are an isolated datum. What emerges here is a part-problem, an aspect of the general problem of civilization at its present stage.

In this case, too, the peculiarity of the present situation may be better seen by reference to an example of the same problem from the past. In late October 1758 the Margravine of Bayreuth, the sister of King

Frederick II of Prussia, lay dying. The King was not able to travel to see her, but sent in haste his own physician Cothenius, in case he could still help. He also sent verses and the following letter, dated 20 October 1758:

> Most tenderly-beloved Sister,
> Receive kindly the verses I am sending you. I am so filled with you, your danger and my gratitude, that your image constantly rules my soul and governs all my thoughts, waking or dreaming, writing prose or poetry. Would that Heaven might grant the wishes of your recovery that I daily send there! Cothenius is on his way; I shall worship him if he can preserve the person who in all the world is closest to my heart, whom I esteem and honour and for whom I remain, until the moment when I too return my body to the elements, most tenderly-beloved sister, your loyal and devoted brother and friend,
> Frederick.

The king wrote this valedictory letter to his sister not in French, but in German, which he did seldom. We can imagine that this letter brought solace to the dying woman and eased her departure from the living – if she was still able to read it.

The German language is not particularly rich in finely shaded expressions for non-sexual emotional attachments between people – non-sexual, whatever their origin may be. Words corresponding to the English 'affection' and 'affectionate' are lacking. *Zuneigung* and *zugetan*, suggesting the idea of 'inclination', do not quite convey the temperate warmth of the English term, and are less commonly used. Frederick's 'most tenderly-beloved sister' is, no

25

doubt, a very exact expression of his feeling. Would it be used today? His attachment to his sister was probably the strongest bond to a woman or to any person in his life. We can assume that the feelings verbalized in this letter are sincere. The affection between brother and sister was reciprocal. He clearly understood that an assurance of his undiminished affection would bring comfort to the dying woman. But the expression of these feelings is clearly made easier for him by his implicit trust in certain linguistic conventions of his society which he allows to guide his pen. The modern reader, with a sharp ear for the clichés of the past, may experience 'your image' that 'constantly rules my soul' as conventional, and 'would that Heaven might grant the wishes' as theatrically Baroque, particularly in the mouth of a monarch not noted for piety. Frederick does indeed use conventional terms to express his feelings. But he is able to use them in such a way that the sincerity of his feelings is apparent, and we may suppose that the recipient of the letter felt this sincerity. The structure of communications was such that those to whom they were addressed could distinguish between sincere and insincere uses of the courtly phrases, while our ears no longer discern these nuances of civility.

This sharply illuminates the present situation. The brief spurt of informalization[7] still in progress makes us especially mistrustful of the ready-made rituals

[7] Cf. Cas Wouters, 'Informalisation and the civilising process', in *Human Figurations. Essays for Norbert Elias*, ed. Peter R. Gleichmann, Johan Goudsblom and Hermann Korte, Amsterdam, 1977, pp. 437–53.

26

and 'flowery' phrases of earlier generations. Many socially prescribed formulae have the aura of past systems of rule about them; they can no longer be used mechanically like the *om mani padme* around the prayer-wheels of Buddhist monks. But at the same time the change accompanying the present stage of civilization produces in many people an unwillingness and often an incapacity to express strong emotions, either in public or in private life. They can only be ventilated, so it seems, in political and social conflicts. In the seventeenth century men could weep in public; today this has become difficult and infrequent. Only women are still able, still socially allowed, to do so — for how much longer?

In the presence of dying people — and of mourners — we therefore see with particular clarity a dilemma characteristic of the present stage of the civilizing process. A shift towards informality has caused a whole series of traditional patterns of behaviour in the great crisis-situations of human life, including the use of ritual phrases, to become suspect and embarrassing for many people. The task of finding the right word and the right gesture therefore falls back on the individual. The concern to avoid socially prescribed rituals and phrases increases the demands on the individual's powers of invention and expression. This task, however, is often beyond people at the current stage of civilization. The way people live together, which is fundamental to this stage, demands and produces a relatively high degree of reserve in expressing strong, spontaneous affects. Often they are able only under exceptional pressure

27

to overcome the barrier blocking actions resulting from strong feelings, and their verbalization. Thus, unembarrassed discourse with or to dying people, which they especially need, becomes difficult. It is only the institutionalized routines of hospitals that give a social framework to the situation of dying. These, however, are mostly devoid of feeling and contribute much to the isolation of the dying.

Religious death rituals can arouse in believers the feeling that people are personally concerned about them, which is doubtless their real function. Apart from these, dying is at present a largely unformed situation, a blank area on the social map. The secular rituals have been largely emptied of feeling and meaning; traditional secular forms of expression lack the power to convince. Taboos prohibit any excessive show of strong feelings, although they may be present. And the traditional aura of mystery surrounding death, with the remnants of magical gestures — opening the windows, stopping the clocks — makes death less amenable to treatment as a human, social problem that people have to solve with and for each other. At present those close to the dying often lack the ability to give them support and comfort by proof of their affection and tenderness. They find it difficult to press dying people's hands or to caress them, to give them a feeling of undiminished protection and belonging. Civilization's overgrown taboo on the expression of strong, spontaneous feelings ties their tongues and hands. And living people may half unconsciously feel death to be something contagious and threatening; they involuntarily draw back from the dying. But, as with every parting of people who are intimate, a gesture of undiminished affection is, for the one taking final leave, perhaps the greatest help, apart from the relief of physical pain, that those left behind can give.

8

THE withdrawal of the living from the moribund, and the silence that gradually spreads around them, are continued when the end has come. This is seen, for example, in the treatment of corpses and in the care of graves. Both have today passed largely out of the hands of the family, relatives and friends, and into the hands of paid specialists. The memory of the dead person may remain fresh; dead bodies and graves as foci of feeling have lost significance. Michelangelo's *Pietà*, the mourning mother with the body of her son, remains comprehensible as a work of art but hardly imaginable as a real event.

How far grave-care has passed from the family to specialists is shown by a brochure issued by cemetery-gardeners.[8] Naturally, it warns against competitors and opponents who might reduce the quantity of flowers adorning graves. We may suppose that the marketing agency has attuned the

---

[8] *Friedhof. Grüner Raum in der Stadt*, published by Zentrale Marketinggesellschaft der deutschen Agrarwirtschaft mbH, in collaboration with Zentralverband Gartenbau e. V. Bundesfachgruppe Friedhofsgärtner.

brochure as closely as possible to the mentality of prospective customers. The silence on the significance of graves as places where dead people are buried is therefore almost total. Understandably, explicit references to any connection between the profession of cemetery-gardener and the burying of corpses are entirely lacking. This careful concealment, which mirrors the mentality of the potential clients, emerges particularly clearly if we recall the tenor of the seventeenth-century poems quoted earlier. The frankness with which they speak of what happens to the body in the grave is in sharpest contrast to the hygienic suppression of distasteful associations from the printed matter and no doubt from the social conversation of our time. That Marvell could hope to win the favour of the adored woman by warning that worms would try her 'long-preserved virginity', and that her 'quaint honour [would] turn to dust' in the grave, gives an indication of how far the threshold of repugnance has advanced since then in the course of an unplanned civilizing process. There, even poets speak unembarrassed of the worms of the grave; here, even cemetery-gardeners avoid anything that might recall the connection between graves and people's deaths. The mere word 'death' is avoided wherever possible; it appears only once in the brochure — when commemoration days for the dead are mentioned; and the bad impression made by the word is at once balanced by the mention of wedding days — when flowers are also needed. The dangerous associations of the cemetery are countered by presenting it simply as a 'green space in the town':

> German cemetery-gardeners . . . would like to give the
> cemetery greater emphasis in public awareness as a
> cultural and traditional area, a place of recollection, and
> as part of urban greenery. For a heightened public aware-
> ness is the best guarantee that the traditional picture of the
> green and blooming cemetery will not one day be
> endangered by alien burial customs, by restrictions based
> on economic arguments, by uncontrolled design running
> riot or by technocratic graveyard planning governed
> solely by rationalization.

It would be rewarding to discuss the tactics of the
struggle against various commercial opponents in
detail, but not here. At any rate, potential clients are
sheltered from the recollection of death and anything
pertaining to it as far as is humanly possible. For the
anticipated clientele death has become distasteful.
But the act of avoidance and concealment in turn has
a somewhat distasteful effect.

It would be a very fine thing if the place of
remembrance of the dead were really set out as a park
for the living. That is the image the cemetery-
gardeners would like to convey — 'a quiet, green,
blooming island amid the hectic noise of daily life'. If
only it were really parks for the living that were
planned, parks where grown-ups were free to eat
their sandwiches and children to play together.
Perhaps that was once possible, but it is forbidden
today by the tendency towards solemnity, the idea
that wit and laughter are unseemly in the vicinity of
the dead — symptoms of the half-unconscious
attempt of the living to distance themselves from the

dead and to push this embarrassing aspect of human animality as far as possible behind the scenes of normal life. Children who tried to play happily around the graves would be scolded by the guardians of the well-trimmed lawns and flowerbeds for their lack of reverence for the dead. But when people have died, they know nothing of the reverence with which they are or are not treated. And the solemnity with which funerals and graves are surrounded, the idea that there should be stillness around graves, that one ought to talk in hushed voices in cemeteries, to avoid disturbing the peace of the dead — all these are really forms of distancing the living from the dead, means of holding at a distance a sense of threat from their proximity. It is the living who demand reverence for the dead, and they have their reasons. These include their fear of death and the dead; but they often also serve as means of enhancing the power of the living.

9

EVEN the way in which the expression 'the dead' is used is curious and revealing. It gives the impression that dead people in some sense still exist, not solely in the memory of the living but independently of them. But the dead do not exist. Or they exist only in the memory of the living, present and future. It is particularly towards the unknown future generations that those now alive turn with all that is meaningful and significant in their achievements and creations. But usually they do not fully realize it. The fear of dying is no doubt also a fear of the loss and destruction of what the dying themselves regard as significant and fulfilling. But only the forum of those who have not yet been born can decide whether what appears significant to earlier generations will also be significant beyond their lives for other people. Even tombstoncs in their simplicity are addressed to this forum — perhaps a passer-by will read on the stone, thought to be imperishable, that here lie buried these particular parents, those grandparents and children. What is written on the unperishing tombstone is a mute message of the dead to whoever is alive — a symbol of a perhaps still unarticulated feeling that the only way in which a dead person lives on is in the memory of the living. When the chain of remembrance is broken, when the continuity of a particular society or of human society itself is ended, then the meaning of everything that its people have done throughout millennia, and of all that has ever seemed significant to them, is also extinguished.

Today it is still somewhat difficult to convey the depth of the dependence of people on each other. That the meaning of everything a person does lies in what he or she means to others, not only to those now alive but also to coming generations, that she or he is therefore dependent on the continuation of human society through generations, is certainly one of the most fundamental of human mutual dependences, those of future on past, of past on future, human beings. But an understanding of this dependence is particularly impeded today by the refusal to look the finitude of individual life, including one's own, and the coming dissolution of one's own person, directly in the face, and to include this knowledge in the way one lives one's life — in one's work, one's pleasure, and above all in one's behaviour towards others.

Too often, people today see themselves as isolated individuals totally independent of others. To further one's own interests — seen an isolation — then seems the most sensible and fulfilling thing for a person to do. In that case, the most important task in life appears to be seeking a meaning for oneself alone, a meaning independent of all other people. No wonder people seeking this kind of meaning find their lives absurd. For the time being, clearly, people can see themselves only with difficulty and infrequently in their dependence on others — a dependence that can be mutual — as limited links in the chain of generations, as torch-bearers running in a relay, who finally pass on to others the torch they have carried forward.

However, the repression and concealment of the finitude of individual human life is certainly not, as it is sometimes presented to be, a peculiarity of the twentieth century. It is probably as old as the consciousness of this finiteness, as the foreknowledge of personal death itself. In the course of biological evolution, we may suppose, there developed in human beings a kind of knowledge that enabled them to relate the end they knew in the case of other creatures — some of which served them as food — to themselves. Thanks to a power of imagination unique among living creatures, they gradually came to know this end in advance as the inevitable conclusion of every human life. But hand in hand with the anticipation of their own end there probably went from early days an attempt to suppress this unwelcome knowledge and overlay it with more satisfying notions. In this the unique human power of imagination came to their aid. The unwelcome knowledge and the concealing fantasies are therefore probably progeny of the same stage of evolution. Today, in possession of an immense store of experience, we can no longer avoid asking whether these complaisant dreams do not in the long run have far more unwelcome and dangerous results for human beings in their communal life than the unvarnished knowledge.

The concealment and repression of death, that is of the unrepeatable finiteness of each human existence, in human consciousness is a very ancient state of affairs. But the mode of concealment has changed in a specific way in the course of time. In earlier periods collective wishful fantasies predominated as the means of coping with the knowledge of death. They still, of course, play an important role today. The fear of one's own transience is alleviated with the aid of a collective wish-fantasy of eternal life in another place. As the management of human fears is one of the most important sources of the power of people over other people, a profusion of dominions have been established, and continue to maintain themselves, on this basis. With the particularly comprehensive spurt of individualization in recent times, personal and relatively private fantasies of immortality are emerging more frequently from the shell of the collective one and are moving into the foreground.[9]

Freud held the view that the psychological agency that he called the 'Id', the most animalistic layer of the psyche, closest to the physis, which he treated almost as a little person, believes itself immortal. But I do not think we can accept this. On the level of the Id a person has no foresight, so no anticipatory knowledge of her or his own mortality. Without this knowledge the compensatory idea of personal immortality cannot be explained: it would have no function. Freud here attributes to the Id-impulses, which are wholly oriented to the here and now, a level of reflection inaccessible to them.

Many other fantasies discovered by Freud are grouped around the image of death. I have already referred to the guilt-feelings, the notion of death as

[9] I have the feeling that Ariès, despite an admirable learning which extends to contemporary immortality-fantasies, does not do justice to the structure of the change with which we are concerned — again, because he lacks theoretical models of long-term processes and thus the concept of an individualization spurt. He writes with noticeable contempt, and almost aversion, of the immortality-fantasies of contemporary people, contrasting them bluntly with what he believes to be the traditional attitude of calm anticipation of death. He quotes approvingly, with a clear side-thrust at his contemporaries, from Solzhenitsyn's *Cancer Ward*: 'They had not', he writes of traditionally minded people, 'rebelled, resisted, boasted that they would never die' (*Studien zur Geschichte*, p. 25). I really do not know whether contemporary people rebel more. Most of the people with immortality-fantasies that I know are well aware that they are fantasies. At any rate, the matter at issue here has a fairly clearly discernible structure. At earlier times, institutionalized collective fantasies guaranteeing the individual immortality had pride of place,

punishment for misdeeds one has committed. How much help can be given to dying people by alleviating deep-seated anxieties about punishment for imagined — often infantile — offences is an open question. The ecclesiastical institution of forgiveness, absolution, shows an intuitive understanding of the frequency with which guilt-anxieties are associated with the process of dying, for which Freud was the first to give a scientific explanation.

It cannot be my task here to trace all the various fantasy-motifs associated with the idea of one's own death and the process of dying. But one cannot entirely overlook the fact that, both in the magical fantasy-world of simpler peoples and in the corresponding individual fantasies of our day, the image of death is intimately bound up with that of killing. Simpler peoples experience the deaths of socially powerful people, at least, as something that someone

and the weight lent to them by institutionalization and group-belief made it almost impossible to recognize these notions as fantasies. Today the power of these collective ideas over people's minds has diminished somewhat, so that individual immortality-fantasies, sometimes recognized as such, tend to move into the foreground. Theoretical models of long-term processes, such as are expressed in the concept of a spurt of increasing individualization, are not dogmas. With their aid one does not need to do violence to observable data, nor is one able to. Such models can be changed; dogmas as theory-substitutes are inflexible. One cannot help feeling regret, given the great wealth of Ariès's knowledge. It would be a fine thing if he could convince himself that preconceived dogmas make scholars blind even to structures that are almost palpably obvious, like that of the transition of immortality-fantasies from a stage where highly institutionalized, collective fantasies predominate, to another, where individual, relatively private immortality-fantasies emerge more strongly.

37

has done to the dead person, as a kind of murder. The survivors' feelings are involved. They do not pose the more detached question of the impersonal *cause* of death. As is always the case when strong emotions are involved, a guilty party is sought. Only when they know who he is can they hope to take revenge and discharge the passions aroused by the death. They cannot avenge themselves on an impersonal cause. Impulses of this kind, which in simpler societies directly guide people's actions and thought, undoubtedly also play a part in the behaviour of adults in more developed societies. But in their case they do not normally have direct control over behaviour. This is still the case with small children, but their physical weakness usually conceals the passionateness of their impulses from adults. Moreover, young children cannot themselves properly distinguish between a wish to act and an act accomplished, between fantasy and reality. Spontaneous upsurges of hatred and death-wishes have for them magical power; the wish to kill kills. Children in our society are often still able to express such wishes openly. 'Then we'll put Daddy in the dustbin,' said a friend's young son with evident relish, 'and shut the lid.' Probably he would have felt guilt if his father had actually gone away. The little daughter of another friend assured everyone who would listen that it was not her fault that her mother was so ill and had to 'be operated'.

Here we encounter a further component of the particular aversion that often overcomes people in the presence of a dying person today, or − this must be added − of the special attraction that dying people, graves and graveyards have for some people. The fantasies of the latter could be approximately summed up in the words, '*I* did not murder them!' On the other hand, the proximity of dying people or graves sometimes arouses not only fears of their own deaths in people, but suppressed death-wishes and guilt-anxieties, summed up roughly in the question, 'Could *I* be guilty of his or her death? Did *I* wish them dead by hating them?'

Even adults in more developed industrial societies have magical levels of experience that are opposed to impersonal, objective explanations of illnesses and deaths. The strength of the shock that the death of a parent often produces in adults is an example of this. It may be partly connected to the deeply rooted identification between children and parents, or between other people with close emotional ties; i.e. it may be connected to the experience of other people as a part or extension of oneself. The feeling about a lost companion that he or she was 'a part of me' is found in relationships of the most diverse kinds – in long-married people, between friends, in sons and daughters. But in the latter the death of a father or mother frequently stirs up buried and forgotten death-wishes with the associated guilt-feelings, and in some cases fear of punishment. The acute intensification of these feelings may weaken the compensatory fantasies of personal immortality.

Such fantasies, as I have said, have grown more frequent in conjunction with the sharper social individualization of recent times. However, highly institutionalized, collective immortality-fantasies undoubtedly live on with only slightly abated vigour in our societies. A perfectly sensible schoolbook describes what people tell children when a person has died:

> 'Your Grandfather is in heaven now' — 'Your Mummy is looking down on you from Heaven' — 'Your little sister is an angel now.'[10]

This example shows how firmly established in our society is the tendency to conceal the irrevocable finitude of human existence, especially from children, with collective wishful ideas, and to secure the concealment by a strict social censorship.

10

IN a different socio-biological area that is also fenced in by a complex structure of social regulations — the area of sexual relationships — a noticeable change has taken place in recent years. In this sphere a number of civilizing barriers that were previously regarded as self-evident and indispensable have been dismantled. Social acceptance of behaviour previously under absolute taboo has become possible. Sexual problems can be discussed publicly on a new level of frankness even with children. The secrecy about sexual practices and

[10] *Religion, Bilder und Wörter*, ed. Hans-Dieter Bastian, Hana Rauschenberger, Dieter Stoodt and Klaus Wegenast, Düsseldorf, 1974, p. 121.

many prohibitions surrounding them which served state or clerical institutions as instruments of rule have given way, to a degree unimaginable in Victorian times, to a more open and pragmatic way of behaving and speaking. The greater openness in this area has led to new problems and a period of experimentation with new solutions, both in social practice and in empirical and theoretical research. Perhaps this will succeed in defining the functions of social regulations within the sexual sphere more exactly – their functions in relation both to individual development and to communal life. But it is already clear that a whole series of traditional sexual regulations, which were formed during the unplanned advance of the civilizing process, had a function only in relation to specific hegemonial groups, to specific power relationships, as between monarch and subject, men and women or parents and children. They appeared as eternal moral commandments as long as one group was firmly established in power, and lost much of their function and plausibility when a somewhat less unequal distribution of power came about. This made it possible to experiment with other canons of behaviour in the sexual field, and thus also with other canons of self-control compatible with a more equally balanced mode of living together, allowing a less frustrating balance between instinct control and instinct fulfilment.

The relaxation of de-functionalized sexual taboos has become particularly noticeable in the education of adolescents and the behaviour of adults towards them. At the start of the century the wall of silence on this matter between adults and children was almost impenetrable. Sexual relationships between adolescents, if discovered, were often severely punished. Sexuality was a sphere of secrecy about which children could talk, at most, among themselves, but seldom with adults, especially parents, and on no account at all with teachers. The severity of the social compulsion to conceal, the heavy social pressure weighing on sexual impulses of unmarried young girls and boys, and the social dangers to which they and, of course, adults themselves were exposed on all sides as soon as they failed to control sexual impulses as the norm-structure required left individuals for a time alone with the often wild and passionate desires of their age, and led to that crisis-ridden form of prolonged puberty, the conflicts and agitation of which were regarded at the time as something ordained by nature. Today it emerges more and more clearly as a form of puberty produced by a transient social code of morality.

In the meantime, the secrecy surrounding the sexual sphere has abated. For parents and teachers it has become more possible, to a degree dependent on age, to talk with children about sexual problems without breaching social taboos or contending with high barriers of personal shame and embarrassment. One no longer needs to ward children off with vague hints or petty lies when they ask where babies come from. In short, in this danger area of human social life – sexuality – the patterns of social control, social practice and personal conscience have changed very considerably in conjunction with each other during this century. A strategy of concealment and repression, particularly in the relationship between groups in position and power and the rising generations, a strategy that appeared to those inured to it as self-evident and necessary to the survival of human society, that is, as moral *per se*, proved in practice to be a functional link within a society based on specific power structures. When these gave way to a less unequal distribution of power — between rulers and ruled, between sexes or generations — the strategy of repression also changed. Order did not give way to chaos when the high tide of Victorian shame and embarrassment surrounding sexual life receded somewhat, and the formalized secrecy yielded to more open speech and behaviour.

11

WITH regard to death, the tendency to isolate and conceal it by turning it into a special area has hardly decreased since the last century, and has possibly increased. It is perhaps only in comparing the different bio-social danger-zones at different stages of social development that one realizes how uneven the rise and decline of taboos, of formalization and informalization may be in these different areas of social life, even though in people's experience dangers from death and from instincts may be intimately connected. The defensive attitudes and the embarrassment with which, today, people often react to encounters with dying and death fully bear comparison with the reaction of people to overt encounters with aspects of sexual life in the Victorian age. As regards sexual life, a limited but noticeable relaxation has set in; social and perhaps individual repression is no longer quite so rigid and so massive as it used to be. But with regard to dying and death, repression and embarrassment have, if anything, increased. Clearly, the resistance to bringing death into the open, into a more relaxed relation to dying, is greater than in the case of sexuality.

One might suppose that differences in the degree of danger experienced play a part here. The danger that unrestrained or over-restrained sexuality represents for people is, one might say, a partial danger. Rapists or sexually frustrated people may pose a threat to others and themselves, but as a rule they do not die from it — life goes on. Compared with this kind of threat, that of death is total. Death is the absolute end of the person. So the greater resistance to its demythologization perhaps corresponds to the greater magnitude of danger experienced.

But on reflecting on such questions we cannot ignore the fact that it is not actually death itself that arouses fear and terror, but the anticipatory image of death. If I were here and now to become painlessly dead, that would not be in the least terrifying for me. I should no longer be here, and consequently could feel no terror. Terror and fear are aroused solely by the image of death in the consciousness of the living. For the dead there is neither fear nor joy.

There is, therefore, a fundamental link between the

two aspects of life discussed earlier. It can be easily overlooked. Both sexuality and death are biological facts that are shaped by experience and behaviour in a socially specific way, i.e. in accordance with the stage reached by the development of humanity, and of civilization as an aspect of this development. Every individual works up the common social patterns in his own way. If we realize that what is decisive for people's relation to death is not simply the biological process of death but the evolving, stage-specific idea of death and the attitude associated with it, the sociological problem of death appears in sharper relief. It becomes easier to perceive at least some of the special features of contemporary societies, and of the associated personality structures, that are responsible for the peculiarity of the death-image, and so for the nature and degree of the social repression of death in more developed societies.

12

THESE special features include, first, the length of individual life in these societies, as already mentioned. In a society with an average life expectancy of seventy-five, death for a person of twenty or even thirty is considerably more remote than in a society with an average life expectancy of forty. It is easy to understand that in the former a person is able to keep the idea of death at a distance for a greater part of his or her life.[11] Even in advanced societies, an objective danger of death is always present, as it must be for all living things. But it can be forgotten. For a considerable sector of these societies death is a good way off. In the other case, in less developed societies with a shorter life expectancy, the uncertainty is greater. Life is shorter, the threat of death is brought more insistently to consciousness, the thought of death is more pervasive, and magic practices to deal with this greater, though mostly hidden, anxiety for the integrity of life and limb, practices that go hand-in-hand with greater insecurity, are widespread.

The second special feature of contemporary societies that is relevant here is the experience of death as the final stage of a natural process, an experience that has gained significance through progress in medical science and in practical measures to raise the standard of hygiene. The idea of an ordered natural process is itself characteristic of a specific stage in the development of knowledge and society. This idea of nature is taken so much for granted in the more developed societies that we are hardly aware of how much our trust in the unshakable laws of nature contributes to the feeling of security in face of natural events that is characteristic of people in scientific societies. Since they take this degree of security for granted, and perhaps think of it as emanating from human rationality, they do not usually comprehend the far greater uncertainty that people of pre-scientific

[11] But perhaps there would be fewer road accidents in these societies if people did not keep it at quite such a distance.

46

societies feel in face of what we — but not they — experience as an impersonal nexus of natural events. The image of death prevalent in more developed societies is heavily influenced by this reassuring knowledge. People know well that death will come; but the knowledge that it is the end of a natural process helps greatly to allay anxiety. The knowledge of the implacability of natural processes is alleviated by the knowledge that, within limits, they are controllable. More than ever before, we can hope today, by the skill of doctors, by diet and by medicaments, to postpone death. Never before in the history of humanity have more-or-less scientific methods of prolonging life been discussed so incessantly throughout the whole breadth of society as in our day. The dream of the elixir of life and of the fountain of youth is very ancient. But it is only in our day that it has taken on scientific, or pseudo-scientific, form. The knowledge that death is inevitable is overlaid by the endeavour to postpone it more and more with the aid of medicine and insurance, and by the hope that this might succeed.

13

CLOSELY bound up with these structural and also experiential characteristics of contemporary societies is a third one that is responsible for common features of the image of death and the attitude towards it — the relatively high degree of internal pacification in these societies. Connected to this is the fact that the people forming these societies usually envisage death in a quite specific form. When they try to imagine this process, they probably think first of a peaceful death in bed resulting from illness and the infirmity of age. This picture of dying that emphasizes the natural character of the process appears as normal, while violent death, particularly at the hands of another person, appears as exceptional and criminal. That physical security from violence by other people is not so great in all societies as in our own is usually not clearly realized.

It is therefore necessary to say that the relatively high degree of protection against violence from other people enjoyed by members of more developed societies, and the treatment of death by violence as something exceptional and criminal, do not arise from a personal insight of the people concerned but from a very specific organization of society – a relatively effective monopolization of physical violence. Such a monopolization cannot be achieved from one day to the next; it results from a long and largely unplanned development. In societies of this kind a point has been reached where rulers permit the use of violence only to specific groups controlled by them. In many cases only they – the police and the armed forces – are entitled without punishment to carry weapons and on certain occasions to use them without being punished. By and large, it is only in the last two or three hundred years that the organization of European states and their descendants has attained the degree and pattern of effective monopoly control of violence that has made possible the relative restraint of passions and relative exclusion of violence from human relationships, which is now taken almost for granted in more developed societies, and to which the human relationships implicit in the production and distribution of goods owe their specific character as economic relationships. For where direct coercion by physical violence determines the production and distribution of goods, in the form of rapine, war and slavery, these processes have not really the character we refer to as economic; they are hardly calculable and lack recurrent quantifiable regularities, the mainstay of the science of economics and inherent in the non-violent 'economy' as a special sphere of society.

In societies without such highly specialized monopoly institutions of physical violence, and particularly in warrior-societies, physical attacks by people on other people are a far more normal part of social life. If not all the members of such societies, then at least those of the upper stratum carry weapons as an indispensable appendage in their dealings with others. Physically weak or disabled people, old men, women and children stay largely within the confines of the house or castle, tribal village or urban quarter inhabited by their own people; they can venture out only with special protection.

The development of the personality structure takes a different direction in such societies from that in highly organized industrial societies. The readiness for attack or defence in physical combat, at least in men, is greater, the expectation of death in a bloody confrontation with other people is more constantly

49

present, the expectation of dying peacefully in bed more exceptional. Here too we see how far personality structures with their attendant conceptions, including the image of death, conceptions that in our own society we are apt to take for granted and perhaps to regard as universal human properties, are in fact influenced by peculiarities of the social structure that have crystallized only very gradually in the course of a long social process.

Nevertheless, even in societies that are highly pacified internally, the expectation of dying in bed is more deceptive than it might at first appear. Quite apart from the fairly high accident and homicide figures, group conflicts drifting towards a violent resolution are increasing in our period, conflicts whose participants believe that they can be settled only by killing opponents and sacrificing members of their own group, and which are usually planned, even in peacetime, as violent life-and-death struggles.

Among the problems of our time that perhaps deserve more attention, therefore, is that of the psychological transformation undergone by people who find themselves removed from a situation in which the killing of other people is strictly forbidden and heavily punished, to a situation where the killing of others, whether by the state, a party or another group, is not merely socially permitted but explicitly demanded.

If we speak of the civilizing process in whose course dying and death are moved more firmly behind the scenes of social life and fenced in by relatively intense feelings of embarrassment and relatively strict verbal taboos, we must qualify this by adding that the experiences of the two great European wars, and perhaps far more of the concentration camps, show the fragility of the conscience that prohibits killing and then insists on the isolation of dying and dead people, as far as possible, from normal social life. The mechanisms of self-constraint that are involved in the repression of death in our societies clearly disintegrate relatively quickly once the external mechanism of constraint imposed by the state — or by sects or combat groups — basing itself on authoritative collective doctrines and beliefs, violently changes course and orders the killing of people. In the two world wars the sensitivity towards killing, towards dying people and death clearly evaporated quite quickly in the majority of people. How the personnel of the concentration camps adjusted psychologically to the daily mass-killings is an open question that would merit closer investigation. It is often obscured by the question of who bears the guilt for such events. But for social praxis, and with a view to preventing such events, the former, more factual question is of special importance. The stereotyped answer to it, 'I was obeying orders', shows to what extent the individual conscience structure was here still dependent on the external constraint mechanism of the state.

14

THE fourth special feature of developed societies that deserves mention as a pre-condition of the peculiarity of their image of death is their high degree and specific pattern of individualization. The image of death in a person's memory is very closely bound up with his image of himself, of human beings, prevalent in his society. In more developed societies people see themselves broadly as fundamentally independent individual beings, as windowless monads, as isolated 'subjects', to whom the whole world, including all other people, stands in the relationship of an 'external world'. Their 'inner world', it seems, is cut off from this 'external world', and so from other people, as if by an invisible wall.

This specific way of experiencing oneself, the self-image of *Homo clausus* characteristic of a recent stage of civilization, is closely linked to an equally specific way of experiencing, in anticipation of one's own death and probably in the actual situation, one's own act of dying. But research into dying — for reasons not unconnected to the social repression — is still in an early stage. Much remains to be done in gaining a better understanding of the experience and needs of dying people and of the connection between such experience and needs and their way of life and self-image. In a veiled form, with the aid of concepts like 'mystery' or 'nothingness', Existentialist writings sometimes project a quasi-solipsistic image of a human being on to death. Much the same can be said of the 'Theatre of the Absurd'. Its exponents, too, start implicitly – and sometimes explicitly – from the assumption that the life of a person, as they understand it – that is, the life of a fundamentally isolated being hermetically sealed from the world – must have a meaning, and perhaps even a pre-ordained meaning, solely in and for itself. Their quest for meaning is a quest for the meaning of an individual person in isolation. When they fail to find this kind of meaning, human existence appears meaningless to them; they feel disillusioned; and the void of meaning thus established for human life usually finds in their eyes its supreme expression in the knowledge that each human being must die.

It is easy to understand that a person who believes himself to be living as a meaningless being, also dies as one. But this understanding of the concept of meaning is as misleading as the image of a human being to which it belongs. The category of 'meaning', too, is here stamped by the image of *Homo clausus*. The peculiar fact that, through the mediation of language, data of every kind, including one's own life, can have meaning for people has for a good while been the subject of copious philosophical reflections. But with very few exceptions, these meditations try to gain access to the problem of meaning by postulating as the 'subject' of meaning – in the traditional philosophical manner – a human individual in a vacuum, an isolated monad, a sealed 'self', and then perhaps, at a higher level of generality, *the* isolated human being, or, as the case may be, consciousness as a universal. Whether expressly or not, it is then expected that each person by himself, precisely as an isolated monad, must have a meaning, and the meaninglessness of human existence is lamented when this kind of meaning is not found.

But the concept of meaning cannot be understood by reference to an isolated human being or to a universal derived from it. What we call 'meaning' is constituted by people in groups who are dependent on each other in this or that way and can communicate with each other. 'Meaning' is a social category; the subject corresponding to it is a plurality of interconnected people. In their intercourse, signs that they give each other — which can be different in each group of people — take on a meaning, to begin with a communal meaning.

Human groups that speak a common language can serve as a basic model, a point of departure for any discussion about problems of meaning. Communication by means of languages is a uniquely human characteristic, unique like a request for meaning. No other living things can communicate in this manner; no others attach learned and group-specific meanings to equally learned and group-specific sensory patterns, used as the dominant means of communication. In all other cases unlearned and species-specific signals dominate communication. To be sure, among humans sound patterns produced by one person can have a 'meaning' for others. But they have a meaning only if — and because — the sender and the receiver have learned to associate with sets of specific sound patterns the same memory images, or in other words the same meaning. In this, the most elementary, form of 'meaning' its social character shows itself very clearly. Thus an English-speaking person can expect that, by producing the sound pattern. 'What time is it?', another English-speaking person will associate with this sensory pattern the same memory image as the speaker does and will respond with an appropriate image-carrying sound pattern such as 'Precisely four-fifteen'. Produced in the streets of Paris the sound pattern 'What is the time?' may elicit no response or a blank stare. The sounds would be meaningless in a different social setting. Every human being becomes bonded to others from early childhood on by learning to use, as a means of sending and receiving messages, a group-specific code of symbols, or in other words a language. Each person may — within limits — vary it individually; but if he or she goes too far in this he/she forfeits — in the present or the future — the communicability of the science and so their meaning.

The meaning of a person's words and the meaning of a person's life have in common that the meaning associated with them by that person cannot be separated from that associated with them by other persons. The attempt to discover in a person's life a meaning that is independent of what this life means for other people is quite futile. In the praxis of social life the connection between a person's feeling and the awareness that it has meaning for other human beings, and that others have a meaning for that life, is easy enough to discover. On this plane we normally understand without difficulty that expressions such as 'meaningful' or 'meaningless', referring to a human life, are closely linked to the significance for others of what that person is and does. But in reflections on the self this understanding easily evaporates. There, the feeling widespread in the more developed societies with their highly individualized members, that everyone exists for himself alone, independently of other human beings and the whole 'external world' usually gains the upper hand, and with it the idea that a person — oneself — must have a meaning entirely on one's own. The traditional mode of philosophizing, built up on this way of experiencing oneself and at the same time one of its most representative manifestations, too often obstructs the inclusion in reflections on higher levels of what is immediately evident on the level of praxis — the participation of a person in a world of other persons and 'objects'.

Every human being lives on 'external' plants and animals, breathes 'external' air and has eyes for 'external' light and colours. He or she is born of 'external' parents and loves or hates, makes friends or enemies of 'external' people. On the level of social praxis all this is known to people as a matter of course. In more detached meditation this experience is often repressed. Members of complex societies then often experience themselves as beings whose 'inner self' is totally separated from this 'external world'. A powerful philosophical tradition has, as it were, legitimized this illusory dichotomy. Discussions about meaning have been profoundly affected by it. 'Meaning' is widely treated as a messenger from an immured individual's 'inner world'.

The resulting distorted self-image of a person as a totally autonomous being may reflect very real feelings of loneliness and emotional isolation. Tendencies of this kind are highly characteristic of the specific personality structure of people of our age in more highly developed societies and of the particular type of high individualization prevailing there. Self-control all round, in that case, is frequently built so firmly into people growing up in these societies that it is experienced as a wall that actually exists, blocking affects and other spontaneous impulses directed towards other people and things, and so cutting them off.

So far the problem of the loneliness of the dying has been considered above all in relation to the attitudes of the living. But this needs to be supplemented. In such societies, understandably, tendencies towards feelings of loneliness and isolation are often present also in the personality structure of the dying people themselves. There are of course always differences related to class, sex and generation. One might suppose such tendencies to be particularly developed in academic circles, in the middle classes generally more than in working classes, in men perhaps more than in women. But this is at present mere guesswork, intended to draw attention to problems that have hardly been touched on, and to say that they have not been forgotten.

All the same, in these evenly pacified societies where communal life demands an all-embracing and even control of all volcanic instinctual impulses, a temperate damping of violent emotions all round,

57

there are certain common features of the personality structure transcending class and other group differences. Admittedly, they emerge clearly only through comparison with societies at a different stage of civilization. These common features include the high degree of individualization, the comprehensive and constant restraint of all strong instinctual and emotional impulses, and a tendency towards isolation, all of which have gone hand in hand with these personality structures up to now.

In the dying, too, this tendency can be discerned. They may resign themselves to it or, just because they are dying, try a last time to breach the wall. However this may be, they need more than ever the feeling that they have not lost their meaning for other people — within limits: too much expression of sympathy may be just as unbearable for them as too little. It would be incorrect to speak of the specific revulsion and reserve induced by civilization in the living towards the dying in societies of our kind without pointing at the same time to the possible embarrassment and reserve of the dying towards the living.

15

THE special nature of dying and of the experience of death in advanced societies cannot be properly understood without reference to the powerful individualization spurt setting in with the Renaissance and, with many fluctuations, continuing until today. In the early phases it finds expression in the idea of contrast between convivial life and solitary death — for example, in the lines of Opitz:

> If I have little to bequeath
> Yet I have a noble wine;
> Will make merry with my fellows
> Even though I die alone. [12]

This 'alone', the idea that one can be merry with others but must die alone, may seem so self-evident today that one is inclined to see in it an experience of people at all times and in all places. But this idea, too, is by no means to be found at all stages of human development. It is much less universal than the endeavours of people to find an explanation of why they must die. This plays a central role in the earliest version of the Sumerian Gilgamesh epics that we possess, from about the beginning of the second millenium BC. By contrast, the idea of having to die *alone* is characteristic of a comparatively late stage of individualization and self-awareness.

This 'alone' points to a whole complex of interrelated meanings. It can refer to the expectation that one can share the process of dying with no one. It can express the feeling that with our death the little world of our own person, with its unique memories and its feelings and experiences known only to ourselves, with its own knowledge and dreams, will vanish for ever. It can refer to the feeling that in dying we are left alone by all the people to whom we feel attached.

[12] Martin Opitz, *Weltliche Poemata 1644*. Oden oder Gesänge XVIII.

However it may be accented, this motif of dying alone occurs more frequently in the modern period than ever before. It is one of the recurrent forms of experience of people in a period when the self-image of a person as a totally autonomous being, not only different from all other people but separated from them, existing entirely independently of them, is becoming ever more clearly marked. The special accent taken on in the modern period by the idea that one dies alone matches the accentuation in this period of the feeling that one lives alone. In this respect too the image of one's own death is closely connected to the image of oneself, of one's own life, and the nature of this life.

Tolstoy, in a short and not very transparent story, 'Master and Man', contrasts the death of a merchant who has risen from the peasantry to that of his peasant servant. The merchant has made something of his life — through his energy, his constant activity, always on the lookout for a good piece of business, always in conflict with competitors who want to snatch it away. Nikita, his servant, whom he provides for while now and then swindling him out of his wages, obeys his orders. He accepts the good and the bad as it comes, for he has no choice. For him there is no way out of this life, no escape — except vodka. He sometimes gets blind drunk. Then he becomes wild and dangerous. Sober, he is patient, obedient, friendly and devoted to his master. They drive out together into a snow flurry with a strong horse before their sledge. A business deal, the purchase of a wood that he does not want to let a competitor have, is awaiting the merchant at a not very distant village. The snowfall gets heavier during the journey. They lose their way and finally, during the night, get stuck in a ravine and are slowly snowed under. They manage to erect, as is the custom, a kind of flag on a long pole so that they can be dug out the next day. Almost to the end the merchant remains very active, as best he can. He dreams of everything he has achieved, and of all he still has to do, rouses himself when he notices that his servant is freezing to death, lies on him with his thick fur coat to keep him warm, slowly falls asleep and freezes to death. Nikita, his peasant servant, submits to death patiently and unresistingly:

> The thought of death, that would probably overtake him this same night, rose up in him, but had nothing painful or terrible for him. This was because he had had few happy feast-days in his life but many bitter weeks, and he was tired of the uninterrupted work.

Tolstoy describes the customary subservience of the working man to his earthly lord — a devotion exceeded only by that of the faithful horse — and so to the Lord in Heaven as well. He therefore tries quite explicitly to make clear the connection between the way a person lives and the way a person dies. [13]

For the master, the merchant struggling to rise, life, and so survival, has a high degree of meaning

[13] To supplement what Ariès says of the serenity of the dying Russian peasant as reflected in Russian literature, this quotation may be of interest. It shows very clearly the connection between the way of living and the way of dying, which Ariès somewhat neglects.

and value. He remains active, and tries to keep his servant and helper alive, till the cold overcomes him. The servant, to whom life gives much work, toil and oppression, but scarcely a task or goal of his own, dreams his way patiently into death, only to escape it — as Tolstoy has it — through the protecting body and warm coat of his master.

The way a person dies depends not least on whether and how far he or she has been able to set goals and to reach them, to set tasks and perform them. It depends on how far the dying person feels that life has been fulfilled and meaningful — or unfulfilled and meaningless. The reasons for this feeling are by no means always clear — that too is an area for investigation that is still wide open. But whatever the reasons, we can perhaps assume that dying becomes easier for people who feel they have done their bit, and harder for people who feel they have missed their life's goal, and especially hard for those who, however fulfilled their life may have been, feel that the manner of their dying is itself meaningless.

Meaningful death, meaningless dying — these concepts, too, open the door to problems that, one might think, receive too little public consideration. To some extent, this may well be because they are easily confused with another problem, almost identical in its formulation but totally different in its meaning. If we wish to say of someone that he occupies himself with something totally useless, we may be saying as an example that he is reflecting on the meaning of life. The uselessness in that case stems from the fact that he is seeking a metaphysical meaning for human life, a meaning that is, as it were, prescribed for the individual, whether by extra-human powers or by nature. But such a metaphysical meaning can at best be the subject of philosophical speculation; one may give one's wishes and fantasies free rein in seeking this kind of meaning – the answers can be no more than arbitrary inventions. Their content can be neither substantiated nor refuted.

But the meaning under discussion here is of a different kind. People experience events that happen to them as meaningful or meaningless, as making sense or as senseless. It is this experienced meaning that is at issue here. If a thirty-year-old man, the father of two small children and husband of a wife whom he loves and who loves him, is involved in a motorway accident with a driver coming the wrong way, and dies, we say it is a meaningless death. Not because the dead man left a prescribed extra-human meaning unfulfilled, but because a life that had no relation to that of the affected family, the life of the other driver, at one stroke, as if from outside and by chance, demolished and destroyed the life, the goals and plans, the happily and firmly rooted feelings of a human being, and thus something that was eminently meaningful for this family. Not only the expectations, hopes and joys of the dead man were destroyed, but also those of the survivors, his children and his wife. For the people who formed this family, this social setting, this human grouping had a function invested with high positive values. If something has such a function for the life of a person and an event furthers or reinforces it, we say it has meaning for her or for him. Conversely, when something that has such a function for a person or group ceases to exist, becomes unrealizable or is destroyed, we speak of a loss of meaning.

The little that it has been possible to say here on the nature of meaning, and so on the 'meaning of a life', may not be entirely without value in understanding a special problem of dying people. The fulfilment of meaning for an individual, as we have seen, is closely related to the meaning one has attained in the course of one's life for other people, whether through one's person, one's behaviour or one's work. Today people try to help the dying above all by alleviating their pain and caring as best they can for their bodily comfort. Through these efforts they show that they have not stopped respecting them as human beings.But in busy hospitals, understandably, this often happens in a somewhat mechanical and impersonal way. Even families are today often at a loss for the right words to use in this relatively unfamiliar situation in order to help the dying person. It is not always easy to show to people on their way to death that they have not lost their meaning for other people.

If this happens, if a person must feel while dying that, though still alive, he or she has scarcely any significance for other people, that person is truly alone. It is precisely this form of loneliness for which there are many examples in our day, some common-place, some extraordinary and extreme. The concept of loneliness has a rather wide spectrum. It can refer to people whose desire for love directed towards others has early on been so injured and disturbed that later they can hardly direct it at others without feeling the blows they received earlier, without feeling the pain that this desire exposed them to in former times. Involuntarily, people so affected withdraw their feelings from others. That is one form of loneliness. Another form of loneliness, which is social in the narrower sense, occurs when people live in a place or have a position that does not allow them to meet others of the kind that they feel they need. In this and many related cases the concept of loneliness refers to a person who for this or that reason is left alone. Such people may live among others, but they have no affective meaning for them.

But that is not all. The concept of loneliness refers also to a person in the midst of many others for whom he or she is without any significance, for whom it is a matter of indifference whether or not this person exists, who have broken the last bridge of feeling between themselves and this human being. Vagrants, meths-drinkers sitting in a doorway unheeded by the passers-by, belong to this group. The prisons and torture-chambers of dictators are examples of this kind of loneliness. The way to the gas-chambers is another. There, children and women, young and old men, were driven naked towards their deaths by people who had broken off every feeling of identity and sympathy. As, in addition, those driven helplessly into death were themselves often thrown together by chance and unknown to each other, each of them, in the midst of people, was in the highest degree lonely and alone.

This extreme example may remind us how fundamental and how incomparable is the meaning of people for people. It also gives an indication of what it means for dying people if — still living — they are made to feel that are already excluded from the community of the living.

16

D EATH is not terrible. One passes into dreaming and the world vanishes — if all goes well. Terrible can be the pain of the dying, terrible, too, the loss of the living when a beloved person dies. There is no known cure. We are part of each other. Collective and individual fantasies surrounding death are often appalling. As a result, many people, especially when they get older, secretly or openly live in terror of death. As much suffering may be caused by these fantasies and the fear of death they engender as by the physical pain of a deteriorating body. To calm these fears, to oppose to them the simple reality of a finite life, is a task that still lies before us. It is terrible when people die young before they have been able to give their lives a meaning and taste the joys of life. It is also terrible when men, women and children roam starving through a barren land where death is in no hurry. There are indeed many terrors that surround dying. What people can do to secure for each other easy and peaceful ways of dying has yet to be discovered. The friendship of those who live on, the feeling of dying people that they do not embarrass the living, is certainly part of it. And social repression, the veil of unease that frequently surrounds the whole sphere of dying in our days, is of little help to people. Perhaps we ought to speak more openly and clearly about death, even if it is by ceasing to present it as a mystery. Death hides no secret. It opens no door. It is the end of a person. What survives is what he or she has given to other people, what stays in their memory. If humanity disappears, everything that any human being has ever done, everything for which people have lived and fought each other, including all secular or supernatural systems of belief, becomes meaningless.

Ageing and Dying: Some Sociological Problems

1

AN experience I had in my younger days has taken on a certain significance for me, now that I am older. I attended a lecture by a well-known physicist at Cambridge. He came in shuffling, dragging his feet, a very old man. I caught myself wondering, Why does he drag his feet like that? Why can he not walk like a normal human being? I at once corrected myself. He can't help it, I told myself. He is very old.

My spontaneous youthful reaction to the sight of an old man is very typical of the kind of feelings aroused today, and perhaps still more in earlier periods, in healthy people in the normal age groups by the sight of old people. They know that old people, even when they are quite healthy, often have difficulty in moving in the same way as healthy people in all other age groups except small children. They know this, but in a remote way. They cannot imagine a situation where their own legs or trunk do not obey the commands of their will, as is normal.

I use the word 'normal' deliberately here. That people grow different in old age is often involuntarily seen as a deviation from the social norm. The others, the normal age groups, often have difficulty in empathizing with older people in their experience of ageing — understandably. For most younger people have no basis in their experience for imagining how it feels when muscle tissue gradually hardens and perhaps becomes fatty, when connective tissue multiplies and cell renewal slows down. The physiological processes are well known to science and in part well understood. There is extensive literature on the subject. Much less understood, and far less frequently touched on in the literature, is the experience of ageing itself. This is a comparatively little discussed topic. It is certainly not without importance for the treatment of the old by those who are not — or not yet — old, and not merely for their medical treatment, to have a closer understanding of the experiential aspect of the process of ageing, and of dying as well. But, as I have mentioned, there are clearly very special difficulties in the way of empathy here. It is not easy to imagine that one's own body, which is so fresh and often so full of pleasant feelings, could become sluggish, tired and clumsy. One cannot imagine it and, at bottom, one does not want to. To put it differently, identification with the ageing and dying understandably poses special difficulties for people of other age groups. Whether consciously or unconsciously, people resist the idea of their own ageing and dying as best they can.

This resistance, this process of repression, is, for reasons I shall come back to, probably more pronounced in developed societies than in less developed ones. Now that I myself am old I know, as it were, from the other side how difficult it is for people, young or middle-aged, to understand the situation and the experience of old people. Many of my acquaintances say to me words of kindness such as: 'Astonishing! How do you manage to keep so healthy? At your age!' or: 'You *still* go swimming? How marvellous!' One feels like a rope-dancer, who is quite familiar with the risks of his way of life and fairly certain that he will reach the ladder at the other end of the rope and come down to earth quietly in his own good time. But the people who are watching him from below know that he might fall from his height at any moment and look at him thrilled and slightly scared.

I recall another experience that can serve as an example of the non-identification of younger people with the old. I was a visiting professor at a German university and was invited to dinner by a colleague who was in the prime of life. There was an aperitif before dinner and he invited me to sit down on a very low, modern canvas seat. His wife called us to the dinner table. I stood up, and he gave me a surprised and perhaps somewhat disappointed look. 'Well, you're still in pretty good shape,' he said. 'Not long ago we had old Plessner here for dinner. He sat on the low seat like you but he couldn't get up again, try as he might. You should have seen him. In the end we had to help him.' And he laughed and laughed: 'Hahahahaha! He couldn't get up again!' My host was shaking with laughter. Evidently in that case, too, identification between the not-old and the old caused difficulties.

The feeling, 'Perhaps I shall be old one day', can be totally lacking. All that remains is the spontaneous enjoyment of one's own superiority, and of the power of the young in relation to the old. The cruelty that finds expression in the mockery of helpless old people, in revulsion from ugly old women and men, was probably considerably greater in earlier times than it is today. But it has certainly not disappeared. It is closely connected to a very characteristic change in interpersonal relations that takes place when people grow old or are on their deathbed: as they grow older they grow potentially or actually less powerful in relation to younger people. They become visibly more dependent on others. The way in which people come to terms, as they grow older, with their greater dependence on others, a decrease of their power potential, differs widely from one person to the next. It depends on the whole course of their life and so on their personality structure. But it is perhaps useful to remember that some of the things old people do, in particular some of the strange things, have to do with their fear of losing power and independence and especially of losing control over themselves.

One of the forms of adaptation to this situation is regression to infantile behaviour. I shall not attempt to decide whether this recurrence of infantile behaviour in old people is simply a symptom of physical degeneration or an unconscious flight from their growing fragility into the behaviour patterns of early childhood. At any rate, it also represents an adaptation to a situation of total dependence which has its own pain but also its gratifications. It is a fact that there are people in many old people's homes today who have to be fed, put on a potty and cleaned like very young children. They also wage their power struggle like young children. A night-nurse who treats them a little roughly may be rung for every hour of the night. This is only one of many examples of how the experience of ageing people cannot be understood *unless we realize that the process of ageing often brings about a fundamental change in a person's position in society, and so in his or her whole relationships to other people.* People's power and status change, whether quickly or slowly, earlier or later, when they reach the age of sixty, seventy, eighty or ninety.

2

THE same is true of the affective aspect of the relationships of ageing and, especially, of dying people to others. My theme and the time available oblige me to confine myself to one aspect of this change, the isolation of ageing and dying people that frequently occurs in our society. As I mentioned at the outset, I am concerned not with the diagnosis of physical symptoms of ageing and dying — what are often, not entirely appropriately, called the objective symptoms — but with diagnosing what ageing or dying people themselves 'subjectively' experience. I should like to supplement the traditional medical diagnosis by a sociological diagnosis, concentrating on the danger of isolation to which the ageing and

72

dying are exposed.

One can notice in this respect a very marked difference between the position of ageing and dying people in present-day industrial societies and in pre-industrial, i.e. medieval or early industrial societies. In pre-industrial societies, where the major part of the population lives in villages and is occupied in cultivating land and tending cattle, that is, where peasants or farm labourers form the largest occupational group, it is the family's concern to take care of the ageing and dying. This may be done in a kindly or a brutal way, but there are also structural features that distinguish ageing and dying in such societies from those in more advanced industrial societies. I shall refer to two of these differences. Old people who are growing physically weaker usually stay within the living-area of the family, if sometimes after considerable struggles with the younger members, and they also usually die within this area. Accordingly, everything to do with ageing and dying takes place far more publicly than is the case in highly urbanized industrial societies, and both are formalized by specific social traditions. The fact that everything happens more publicly within the domain of the extended family, in some cases including the neighbours, does not necessarily mean that ageing and dying people experience nothing but kindliness. It is doubtless not uncommon for the younger generation, on coming into power, to treat the older one badly, perhaps even very cruelly. It is not the state's affair to worry about such things.

Today in industrialized societies the state protects

the aged or dying person, like every other citizen, from obvious physical violence. But at the same time people, as they grow older and weaker, are isolated more and more from society and so from the circle of their family and acquaintances. There is an increasing number of institutions in which only old people, who did not know each other in their earlier years, live together. Even with the prevalent high degree of individualization, most people in our society have before retirement formed affective ties not only within their families but with a larger or smaller circle of friends and acquaintances. Ageing itself usually brings with it an increasing withering of such ties outside the narrowest family circle. Except in the case of old married couples, admission to an old people's home usually means not only the final severing of old affective ties, but also means living together with people with whom the individual has had no positive affective relationships. Physical care by doctors and nursing personnel may be excellent. But at the same time the separation of the old people from normal life, and their congregation with strangers, means loneliness for the individual. I am here concerned not only with sexual needs, which may be quite active into extreme old age, particularly among men, but also with the emotional valencies between people who enjoy being together, who have a certain attachment to each other. Relationships of this kind, too, usually diminish with the transfer to an old people's home and seldom find a replacement there. Many old people's homes are therefore deserts of loneliness.

3

THE special nature of dying in developed industrial societies, with emotional isolation as one of its most prominent features, emerges particularly clearly if procedures and prevalent attitudes relating to death in later-stage societies are compared with those in less developed countries. Everyone is familiar with pictures from earlier periods, showing how whole families – women, men and children – gather around the bed of a dying matri- or patriarch. That may be a romantic idealization. Families in that situation may often have been scornful, brutal and cold. Rich people perhaps did not always die quickly enough for their heirs. Poor people may have lain in their filth and starved. It can be said that before the twentieth century, or perhaps before the nineteenth, the majority of people died in the presence of others if only because people were less accustomed to living and being alone. There were not many rooms where a person *could* be alone. Dying and dead people were not as sharply isolated from communal life as is usually the case in societies at later stages. Societies as such were poorer in earlier days; they were not so hygienically organized as later societies. The great epidemics frequently overwhelmed European countries; since at least the thirteenth century, they came and went usually several times in each century up to the twentieth, when people had at last learned how to cope with major plagues.

4

IT is often difficult for people of a later century to put themselves in the place of people living in an earlier one, so that later people cannot properly understand their own situation, or themselves, either. The situation is simply that the social stock of knowledge relating to illness and its causes was in earlier societies, the medieval for instance, not only far more limited, but also far less secure than today. When people lack secure knowledge of reality, they are themselves less secure; they are more easily excited, quicker to panic; they fill the gaps in their realistic knowledge with fantasy-knowledge and seek to appease their fear of inexplicable dangers by fantasy means. So people of former times sought to counter the recurrent epidemics with amulets, sacrifices, accusations against well-poisoners, witches or their own sinfulness, as a means of pacifying their excited feelings.

It may, of course, still happen today that people suffering from an incurable illness, or for other reasons close to death, hear an inner voice whispering that it is the fault of their relatives or punishment for their own sins. But today such private fantasies are less likely to be mistaken for factual public knowledge; they are normally recognizable as private fantasies. Knowledge of the causes of illnesses, of ageing and dying, has become more secure and comprehensive. The control of the great fatal epidemics is only one of many examples of how the growth of reality-congruent knowledge has played a part in changing human feeling and behaviour.

5

PERHAPS it is somewhat misleading to call this receding of emotive fantasy-explanations or, to use Max Weber's rather emotive formula, this 'disenchantment of the world', a process of rationalization. However this term is used, it suggests that it is finally human 'reason' that has changed; it appears to imply that people have become more 'rational', or in plain language more sensible, than in former times. This is a self-valuation that hardly does justice to the facts. One begins to understand the change referred to by the concept of rationalization only if one recognizes that one of the changes involved in it is the growth of fact-oriented social knowledge, knowledge capable of giving a sense of security. The expansion of reality-knowledge and the corresponding contraction of fantasy-knowledge go hand in hand with the increase in effective control of events that can be of use to people, and of dangers that threaten them. Age and death are among the latter. We come across a curious state of affairs if we try to understand what significance the growth of more realistic knowledge in these areas has for humanity's chances of controlling them.

Society's stock of knowledge in relation to the biological aspects of ageing and dying has greatly increased in the last two centuries. Knowledge itself in these areas has become better founded and more realistic. And our powers of control have grown with this increase in knowledge. But on this biological level we now appear to approach an absolute barrier when attempting to extend human control over the processes of ageing and dying still further. This reminds us that here and there the power of human beings in relation to the natural universe has its limits.

Progress in biological knowledge has made it possible to increase the life expectancy of the individual considerably. But however we try, with the aid of medical progress and the increased power of extending the individual's life and alleviating the pains of ageing and dying, a person's death is one of the events that indicates that the increase in human control of nature can have limits. No doubt the scope for such control is in many areas inconceivably large. That does not mean that there are no limits to what is achievable by human beings on the level of natural events.

As far as can be seen, this does not apply to the social plane of human life. Here, no absolute limits to the achievable are in sight, and it is not probable that any will be encountered. But in extending the sphere of their knowledge and control, people certainly do come up against difficult hurdles, barriers that may hold them back for hundreds or even thousands of years, even though they are in no way absolutely inaccessible to human control. Absolute barriers to feasibility exist on the pre-human levels of the cosmos, which we call 'Nature', but on the human—

social levels, referred to by words like 'society' and 'individual' only in so far as they too contain and are built into the unteachable levels of nature.

I shall mention in passing two of the barriers that are currently offering serious obstacles to human orientation and to people's control of their own affairs, although they are by no means insurmountable. First, there is the scale of values commonly seen as self-evident, whereby 'Nature', i.e. pre-human natural events, comprises a sphere valued far more highly than 'culture' or 'society', the area formed and created by human beings themselves. The eternal order of 'nature' is admiringly contrasted to the disorder and mutability of the human world. Many people continue as adults to seek someone to take them by the hand like a child, a mother- or father-figure to show them the way they should go. 'Nature' is one of these figures. It is supposed that everything she does, everything that is 'natural', must be good and salutory for human beings. The harmonious regularity of Newton's picture of 'Nature' found expression in Kant's admiration of the eternal laws of the starry sky above us, the eternal moral laws within us. But Newton's beautiful image of 'Nature' is now behind us. We easily forget that the concept of 'Nature' is now synonymous with what cosmologists conceive as the evolution of the universe, with its purposeless expansion, the production and destruction of countless suns and galaxies, and with the 'black holes' that devour light. Whether we describe this as 'order' or 'chance' and 'chaos', it comes to the same thing.

Nor does it make much sense to say that natural events are good for people or, for that matter, bad. 'Nature' has no intentions; it knows no goals; it is entirely purposeless. The only creatures in this universe that can set goals, who can create and give meaning, are human beings themselves. But it is no doubt still unbearable for many people to imagine that the burden of deciding which goals humanity should pursue, which plans and actions have or have not meaning for human beings, falls on themselves. They constantly seek someone to take this burden from them, someone who prescribes rules by which they should live and sets goals that make their lives worth living. What they expect is a pre-ordained meaning coming from outside; what is possible is a meaning created by themselves and ultimately by human beings together, which gives their life its direction.

The growing-up of humankind is a difficult process. The learning period is long; grave mistakes are inevitable, and the danger of self-destruction, of the annihilation of our own conditions of life, in the course of this learning process is great. But this danger is only increased by people remaining in the attitude of children for whom someone else does everything that only they can do. The idea that nature, if only it is left to itself, will do what is right for humans, including their communal life, is an example. It shows how decisions that only human beings can take, and the responsibility that goes with them, are pushed on to an imaginary mother-figure, 'Nature'. But left to itself nature is full of perils. To be sure, the human exploitation of nature also implies great dangers. But human beings can learn from their mistakes. Extra-human natural processes are incapable of learning. Certainly, human society itself is a stage in the development of nature. But it is distinguished from all previous stages in that human beings can change their behaviour and feelings as a result of common and personal experiences, that is, of learning processes, to a far greater extent, and in a different way, than other creatures. This capacity for change might be of extraordinary value to human beings. But their longing for immortality constantly misleads them into according to symbols of immutability, for example 'Nature' imagined as unchanging, far higher value than to themselves, to the development of their own communal life, and to the changing range and pattern of their control over 'Nature', over 'society' and over their own persons. Perhaps even in reading this one feels a trace of resistance to the revaluation demanded by this exploration. That is one of the obstacles I referred to.

The second hurdle that I shall mention as an example is connected with the present incapacity of people to recognize that, within the sphere of reality that they themselves form together with others, changes that are long-term and unplanned, but that have a specific structure and direction, are taking place, and that these processes, like uncontrollable natural processes, are pushing them involuntarily in one direction or another. Because they do not recognize these unplanned social processes as such and therefore do not know how to explain them, they have

81

no appropriate means of influencing or controlling them. One example of this barrier is the present incapacity of people to recognize the unplanned processes by which they are driven to war over and over again. [1] A large number of states have reached a stage of civilization at which the killing of others does not give their members especial pleasure, nor does their own death in war appear particularly honourable. All the same, people are just as helplessly exposed to the danger of war today as were people at earlier stages of development to uncontrollable flooding by large rivers, or to the great infectious epidemics that sometimes killed a considerable part of a country's population.

I have already spoken of the conceptualization of the relationship of extra-human nature to these human—social processes in terms of opposites like 'Nature' and 'culture', with a decidedly higher valuation of the former. It is not always easy to convince people of the late twentieth century that 'Nature' in its raw state is not particularly well-matched to human needs. Only when primeval forests were cleared, when wolves, wildcats, poisonous snakes, scorpions — in short, all the other creatures that could threaten people — had been exterminated, only when 'Nature' had been tamed and fundamentally transformed by humans, did it appear to populations living largely in towns as being

[1] I can only mention in passing here that the figuration dynamics of free competition between states and which I discussed in terms of a 'monopoly mechanism' in the second volume of my book *The Civilizing Process* plays a decisive role in the drift towards war.

benign towards humanity and beautiful. In reality, natural processes take their course, blindly dispensing good things and bad, the joys of health and the raging pains of illness, to human beings. The only creatures who, when it is necessary, can master, up to a point, the senseless course of nature and help each other are human beings themselves.

Doctors can do so; or at least they can try. But perhaps even they are still partly influenced by the idea that the natural processes are all that matter in their patients. That can sometimes be the case. But sometimes not. Rigid doctrines are of little help here. What is decisive is undogmatic knowledge of the benign and the malignant in nature. At present, medical knowledge is often equated solely with biological knowledge. But it is possible to conceive that, in the future, knowledge of the human person, of people's relations to each other, of their bonds to each other and thus the pressures and constraints they exert on each other, will likewise be a part of medical knowledge.

To this branch of knowledge belong the problems I am discussing here. It is possible that the social aspects of people's lives, their relations to others, have special importance for ageing and dying people just because blind and uncontrollable natural processes have so clearly gained power over them. Yet the knowledge that people have reached the limit of their control over natural processes frequently gives rise, in doctors and perhaps in relations and friends of the ageing and dying person, to an attitude that is in contraction to the latter's social needs.

83

People seem to tell themselves there is nothing they can do, shrug their shoulders and regretfully go on their way. Doctors in particular, whose profession is to gain control over the blind destructive powers of nature, often seem to watch with a shudder how in sick and dying people such blind forces break through the normal self-regulation of the organism and proceed wholly unchecked to destroy the organism itself.

Of course, it is not easy for people to witness this process of decay with equanimity. But perhaps people in this situation have a special need of other people. Signs that the bonds have not yet been severed, that those leaving the human circle are still valued within it, are especially important since they are now weak and perhaps only a shadow of what they were. But for some of the dying it may be right to be alone. Perhaps they are able to dream and do not want to be disturbed. One must sense what they need. Dying has become more informal in our day, and the scope for individual needs, if they are known, greater.

6

ALL this perhaps makes it clearer that the attitudes towards dying and death now prevalent are neither unalterable nor accidental. They are peculiarities of societies at a particular stage of development and so with a particular structure. Parents in these societies are often more reticent than earlier in talking to their children about death and dying. Children can grow up without ever having seen a dead body. At earlier stages of development the sight of corpses was usually far more commonplace. Since then, extension of the average life-span has made death far more remote than it used to be from young people and from living people in general. Obviously, in a society with an average life expectancy of thirty-seven or forty the thought of death is far more immediately present, even for the young, than in a society with a life expectancy of about seventy. It may well be that the understandable horror of atomic war is reinforced by the fact that young people in our society can normally expect a longer life than ever before. I saw it more clearly when a twenty-year-old journalist who was interviewing me frowningly asked, with regard to my book on the 'loneliness of the dying', 'Whatever made you write about such a curious subject?'

All of this plays a part in pushing dying and death further than ever out of sight of the living and behind the scenes of normal life in more developed societies. Never before have people died as noiselessly and hygienically as today in these societies, and never in social conditions so much fostering solitude.

7

IN a well-known book by B. G. Glaser and A. L. Strauss, *Time for Dying*, (Chicago, 1968), the authors make the following observation:

> Most patients belong to a family. If relations appear at the bedside of a dying family member during the last days, their presence can pose serious problems for the doctors and nursing staff of the hospital, and can even reduce the efficiency of patient care. (p. 151)

This brief statement points to a grave, unresolved conflict in the ostensibly rational institutionalization of dying — at least in American hospitals, to which the observations of Glaser and Strauss no doubt primarily refer. The dying person receives the most advanced, scientifically based medical treatment available. But contacts with the people to whom he or she is attached, and whose presence can be of utmost comfort to a person taking leave of life, are frequently thought to inconvenience the rational treatment of the patient and the routine of the personnel. Accordingly, these contacts are reduced or prevented wherever possible. Glaser and Strauss point out in the same context (p. 152) that in some economically less developed regions close relations offer comfort and care to the dying by tradition. They thereby release nursing staff for other tasks. They also take over routine care of patients who are recovering. The personnel are therefore accustomed to their presence.

Relations themselves in need of consolation can help each other. This contrasts clearly to what, according to Glaser and Strauss, takes place in hospitals in more developed countries, where the personnel may have to spend their time comforting distressed relatives.

The picture of this difference is vivid. On one hand the older type: family-members crowd around the stricken person, bring food, administer medicine, clean and wash the patient and perhaps, bringing some of the dirt from the street to the sickbed, tend the patient with unwashed hands. Possibly they hasten the end, for all this is not particularly hygienic. Possibly their presence delays death, for it can be one of the last great joys for dying people to be cared for by family members and friends – last proof of love, a last sign that they mean something to other people. That is a great support – to find a resonance of feeling in others for whom one feels love or attachment, whose presence arouses a warm feeling of belonging. This mutual affirmation of people through their feelings, the resonance of feeling between two or more people, plays a central part in giving meaning and a sense of fulfilment to a human life – reciprocal affection, as it were, to the last.

One should have no illusions: families in less developed states are often anything but harmonious. They often go hand in hand with far greater inequalities of power between men and women and between young and old. Their members may love or may hate each other, perhaps both at the same time. There may be relationships of jealousy and contempt.

Only one thing is rarely to be found on this level of social development, especially in cases where women, the mothers, form the affective integrating centre of the family: there is no emotional neutrality within this extended family framework. In a way, this may come to the aid of the dying. They take leave of the world publicly, within a circle of people most of whom have a strong emotive value for them, and for whom they themselves have such value. They die unhygienically, but not alone. In the intensive care unit of a modern hospital, dying people can be cared for in accordance with the latest bio-physical specialist knowledge, but often neutrally as regards feeling; they may die in total isolation.

8

MOREOVER, the technical perfection of the prolongation of life is certainly not the only factor contributing to the isolation of the dying in our day. The greater internal pacification of developed industrial states and the marked advance of the embarrassment threshold in face of violence gives rise in these societies to a usually tacit but noticeable antipathy of the living towards the dying — an antipathy that many members of these societies cannot overcome even if they cannot approve it. Dying, however it is viewed, is an act of violence. Whether people are the perpetrators or whether it is the blind course of nature that brings about the sudden or gradual decay of a human being is ultimately of no great importance to the person concerned. Thus, a higher level of internal pacification also contributes to the aversion towards death, or more precisely towards the dying. So does a higher level of civilizing restraint. There is no shortage of examples. Freud's protracted death from cancer of the larynx is one of the most telling. The growth became more and more ill-smelling. Even Freud's trusted dog refused to go near him. Only Anna Freud, strong and unwavering in her love for the dying father, helped him in these last weeks and saved him from feeling deserted. Simone de Beauvoir described with frightening exactness the last months of her friend Sartre, who was no longer able to control his urinary flow and was forced to go about with plastic bags tied to him, which overflowed. The decay of the human organism, the process that we call dying, is often anything but odourless. But developed societies inculcate in their members a rather high sensitivity to strong smells.

All these are really only examples of how we have failed to come to terms with the problems of the dying in developed societies. What I have said here is merely a small contribution to the diagnosis of problems that still have to be solved. This diagnosis, it seems to me, ought to be developed further. By and large, we are not yet fully aware that dying in more developed societies brings with it special problems which have to be faced as such.

The problems I have raised here are, as you may see, problems of medical sociology. Present-day medical measures relate mainly to individual aspects of the physiological functioning of a person — the heart, the bladder, the arteries and so on — and as far as these are concerned medical technique in preserving and prolonging life is undoubtedly more advanced than ever before. But to concentrate on medically correcting single organs, or areas of organs that are functioning more and more badly, is really worthwhile only for the sake of the person within whom all these part-processes are integrated. And if the problems of the individual part-processes cause us to forget those of the integrating person, we really devalue what we are doing for these part-processes themselves. The decay of persons that we call ageing and dying today poses for their fellow human beings, including doctors, a number of unperformed and largely unrecognized tasks. The tasks I have in mind here remain concealed if the individual person is considered and treated as if he or she existed solely for her- or himself, independently of all other people. I am not quite sure how far doctors are aware that a person's relationships to others have a co-determining influence both on the genesis of pathological symptoms and on the course taken by an illness. I have here raised the problem of the relationship of people to the dying. It takes, as you see, a special form in more developed societies, because in them the process of dying is isolated from normal social life to a greater degree than it was earlier. A result of this isolation is that people's experience of ageing and dying, which in earlier societies was organized by traditional public institutions and phantasies, tends to be dimmed by repression in later societies. Perhaps, in pointing to the loneliness of the dying, one makes it easier to recognize, within developed societies, a nucleus of tasks that remain to be done.

I am aware that doctors have little time. I also know that people and their relationships are given more attention by them now than they were earlier. What does one do if dying people would rather die at home than in hospital, and one knows that they will die more quickly at home? But perhaps that is just what they want. It is perhaps not yet quite superfluous to say that care for people sometimes lags behind the care for their organs.

Index

public nature of death in past, 16, 18–19, 73, 75, 88
punishment
  after death, idea of, 15–16
  idea of death as, 9–11, 37, 76

repression
  of ageing, 69–70
  of death, 1, 8, 9–12, 16, 18, 34–5, 44–5, 51, 67, 85, 91

rituals
  need for new, 24, 26–7
  religious, 5–6, 28
  secular, 28

Sartre, Jean-Paul, 89
security, relative, of life, 7–8

sexual behaviour, removal of taboos on, 40–3, 44
social problem, death as, 2–5, 11, 28, 45
Solzhenitsyn, A., 36n
stage-specific, ideas of death as, 5, 20–3, 24, 44–6, 84
state as protector of aged and dying, 73–4

taboos on death, 20, 28, 43–5, 51
Tolstoy, L., 60–2

violence, death by, 48–51, 88

Weber, Max, 77
Wouters, Cas, 26n

95